T0208229

The right way, the wrong way or your way?

KATY HANDLEY

authorHOUSE®

AuthorHouse™ UK Ltd.
500 Avebury Boulevard
Central Milton Keynes, MK9 2BE
www.authorhouse.co.uk
Phone: 08001974150

First published by AuthorHouse 03/08/2011

ISBN: 978-1-4567-7301-4 (sc)

Contents

For Adrian and our girls…

Dedicated to the one I love with all my heart that makes each and every one of my dreams come true.

To our three girls Harriett, Lily and Sophia who make us smile everyday without question, reminding us that love really does know no bounds.

Acknowledgements

There really are too many wonderful people to thank, without whom; my world really does not function. But I would like to say a special thank you to the ever inspirational Rosies in our lives that always come to our rescue.

To my rock of support Rebs, who is forever there for me and our family through the good, the bad and those oh so crazy moments we all have like sitting down to write a book with a newborn baby in the house!!!

Not forgetting though, the fabulous Tim, who entertains us all and gives Adrian some sanity in a house full of girls, but who is only just a little scared of tiny people.

Mostly though I would like to thank those of you that make my entire world the way it is; you know who you are and I am truly indebted to you all.

With all my love to you all

XXX

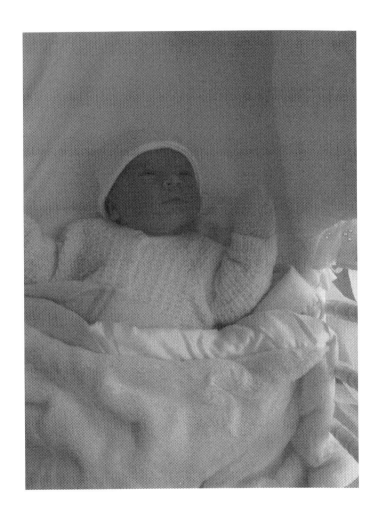

Preface

So go on, go to the kitchen and grab the pack of choccie biccies that you have been hiding, pretending to be on a diet, or as the Health Visitor calls it 'smart healthy eating'. Get your strong black coffee; as that's what we all really crave when we've got kids and get comfy.

Imagine I'm there, right in front of you sat in your lounge having a coffee and this is the chat you've been longing for as a new Mum. I'm no authority on children or families and believe me ours is far from perfect. We've just done it three times now, yes I know a little scary, three children and even more scary all girls. Think of the teenage hormones…that will definitely be a whole book in itself.

Over the years, my partner and I have made loads of mistakes along with a few good decisions and we've muddled through the rest of the way. The only difference between me and everyone else; isn't that I know more, or even less than everyone else about children, it is that I've actually written it down. We all say they should come with a manual and this is my attempt for my friends.

Hopefully over time you'll find your own way, as that's what we all really wish for each other and this will just be an interesting read. You may find a couple of interesting hints and tips though whilst you're meandering through this manual to assist you in the crazy journey of parenthood.

No-one wants to admit to not knowing what they're doing, as that is almost like admitting to failing as a Mum before you even begin, but in reality none of us know the right way to do it, not even the professionals. They don't go home with your child every day, so the theory may be all well and good when sat in the hospital or an office but, when push comes to shove, we all listen to the right way and read the self help books and then just go with what works for our family. We find that right way for ourselves merely by accident, through a lot of trial and a few errors.

All children are vastly different and learn far too early on how to manipulate Mum, so with the best will in the world the theory can't always be applied, even to a text book case. Don't set yourself up for failure by expecting to follow any book to the letter. Take the advice that is useful for your family and forget the rest. You really do not have time to beat yourself up over feeding baby a shop bought organic meal, rather than a homemade one.

None of what I'm writing is gospel and I'm sure all the Health professionals out there are up in arms about my book, but actually what is the big secret? Why do we feel like failures if we do it differently? Why do we feel like we have to hide the truth? Why can't we feel it's okay to be honest about how we actually do cope with our children? So what if it's not the Governments way or your GP's way, does it really matter?

The NHS health professionals may not necessarily approve of my book and child advisors will definitely have raised eyebrows, but they don't go home to the sleepless nights or the incessant crying for no apparent reason. They only get a snap shot of your little monster. Why not muddle through to your own way and be proud of it? As long as all the needs of the children are being met and are in no way facing any harm or danger and are in a loving environment then why not? Why not find your own way? I keep asking that question to anyone who'll listen, but why has no-one got the answer to date?

Rest assured though, I'm not writing this manual for that handful of desperate parents who don't know which way to turn and may possibly be encountering impaired decision making for one reason or another. This book is for everyday people like me and you who are sensible most of the time and have had our worlds turned upside down by the new addition to the family. It's for those of us who are just after a little re-assurance that they're not the only ones that are more than a little unsure about what to do with babies, toddlers and children. It's for those that need a little guidance in general on how the idea of a baby actually rolls out in practice and fits in with everyday life in the modern world.

Don't expect any fancy jargon or a magic wand as no-one can solve your issues with your child apart from you. This book is just a handful of notes on how it's been for me and my family so far, and I'm happy to share that with you guys and anyone else who fancies a read, as to me I honestly don't see why I should keep it a secret.

The Beginning

This manual purely came about by accident; it was never a grand plan. Initially I started noting down short little hints and tips and short cuts that can be made for my friends at their request. This may seem odd, but it was because I was the first, at the age of twenty four a big career girl (or so I thought), to have children in our social circle. That's why so many are now getting inquisitive, as they're now starting out on families of their own. After three for some reason, they seem to think I know what I'm doing. Even today I still laugh out loud at this.

Our friends were sadly mistaken into thinking we were those cool parents getting it all right through a simple day out. This is the predominant reason they all seemed to get a little misled. Being relatively young we took our first born, Harriett, on a fabulous summer pub crawl with our friends when she was only a few months old. Halt the shock horror as it was not in the 18 year old student sense, drunken falling over, but in the sense of a pleasant afternoon with friends outside in the garden of a variety of wine bars and pubs. Harriett just cooed beautifully at our friends and smiled; almost as though joining in the conversation too and then she slept peacefully in her pushchair when nap time came about. Schedules have a lot to answer for and be so so grateful for.

Little did everyone know I was actually on non-alcoholic beer the entire time and just drinking in the banter in the fresh summer air enjoying the sun (albeit Harriett was under the umbrella the entire time wearing factor 50). It was at that point that many of our friends realised that a baby can fit in with their lifestyles and having a baby doesn't stop you enjoying a Sunday at the pub, you just do it in a different way. You don't suddenly become a recluse; you can stay in touch with your friends even if baby is with you.

So that's how for us, our friends realised it wasn't quite so terrifying after all. We just muddled through and let Harriett slot in with us and all the things we still enjoyed, like afternoons in the sun, going out for breakfast on a Sunday and just chilling with friends. The only thing socially that really changed was that the alcohol levels dropped significantly, but the fun stayed the same and a long walk on the beach in the evening really is just as relaxing after work as unwinding in the bar or in front of the TV. As long as the nap time was carefully planned in, as a grumpy baby is enough to heighten anyone's blood pressure, life carried on.

The reason why they're all turning to me now is because we don't seem to have lost our minds just yet and our kids seem to be confident, outgoing and happy. They definitely do have their moments but more importantly they're relaxed children and very sociable with adults as well as their peers. Mostly though they have manners (thankfully) and they always say 'excuse me please' before interrupting and they love sitting at the dining table lunching with us all as much as playing ball or making dens in the garden.

The world of children and babies is a constant minefield and we've only got here by chance, not knowing at the time that the decisions we were making were good ones. We just hoped that they were and there are thousands of decisions and so much choice everyday from which cot is the best? To do we need an all terrain pushchair or a stroller? Or would a Montessori nursery suit our baby's needs? Which car will fit all the car seats in the back? Which vegetables have the most iron? Is the food too lumpy? This is all before the battlefield of schools, headache of friendships and the soul destroying decision of which name! We've all joked that babies should come with a manual and that's what I've done, I've put my baby notes together in an easy to use and easy to read format for those who are just finding their way.

There's no definitive way of doing things, but this is what has worked for our family and hopefully it may assist you in some of the bonkers decision making we were forced to make as parents. Much of the advice and help which is widely available targets the pre-natal area or troublesome toddlers but why should we feel embarrassed when your holding your newborn for the first time and it dawns on you, that you don't know how to change a nappy; I mean why would you as you've never needed to know until this moment. The other time that's almost a light bulb moment, is when you get home with your precious little bundle and you realise that you have spent nine months creating the most perfect organic and stimulating nursery upstairs but where do you put the baby when you're sat downstairs having a coffee? Its little quandaries like this that I'm going to address, as we shouldn't feel embarrassed about any of these situations. We've all been there and yes, it was me not knowing how to change a nappy.

What no-one tells an expectant or new mother is that it doesn't get easier, the issues just change and they definitely do not tell you that you never and I mean never catch up on the missed sleep. You just learn to cope with less and as soon as you admit to yourself, that accepting all help and every babysitting offer, isn't a weakness or failure that it's actually the smart thing to do, the more relaxed you'll be as a parent. No one gets a medal for doing it all on their own, but exhausted parents make bad decisions and have little patience when it comes to even the smallest of things, like spilling a beaker of juice at the dining table for the fourth time after you've said 'be careful'. No-one gets it all right, no-one's super mum, we all need to find our own way of what works and what doesn't for own children and our own lifestyle and where our patience and boundaries truly lie and what shortcuts are acceptable to us.

PART ONE

How It All Began

My First Tips – The First Draft

So here goes guys…my biggest tip is let somebody else do it.

My First Tips – Take Two

Of course I'm only joking; children are one of the most precious gifts and my guess is we only get about 25 percent of it right and if we manage that then we're definitely doing a good job. Firstly, just forget everyone else and focus on yourself and your family and if that means telling mums and sisters to back off then so be it. This is your family and so it should be your way and it's your path to find together as a unit not how everyone else thinks you should do it.

There are hundreds of books targeting what equipment to buy etc so I'm not going to re-iterate what they say, I'm just going to highlight a few essential areas, but just remember you don't need even half of it and the money's better in the bank till baby arrives and see what you really need then. All three of my girls had a changing mat on top of a chest of drawers upstairs rather than an overly priced specially designed table. What use is a changing station when they're six years old? And do you really need a baby wipe warmer, what's wrong with the radiator? Or the hall light rather than that cutesy £80 night light that plays lullabies that actually encourages baby to play not sleep…just switch on the iPod if you really must send baby to sleep with music but remember, if you forget it when on holiday you'll have a fortnight of sleepless nights so only introduce what you can sustain night after night.

The same goes for soothers and mobiles. If you can afford everything though then go for it, I would have loved all those pretty finishing touches and glamorous accessories but I knew for us it was a compromise; we couldn't have everything not only because we couldn't afford it, but where do you actually store it all? Much of the stuff I bought for Harriett I gave away anyway, as it was that useless or I never, and I mean never, used it. You only need to ask yourself 'does baby actually need it when baby arrives?' If the answer is 'no or maybe', then wait awhile and come back to it when baby's at home settled.

For baby's first few days I do have some very important advice though, well I think it's important as no-one told me any of this but its common sense really. However few people rarely even think about it at all so keep reading!

The Beginning – The bits they really didn't tell you

Well here it is, you've got your newborn baby home from hospital safe and sound which is a small triumph in itself it seems, but then it all begins. Where do you put the baby once it wakes up? Upstairs in the crib seems such a long way away now and would you even hear your little darling through those now seemingly vast brick walls? These are all questions those new to parenthood ask themselves. It's exactly the same question you ask yourselves now you've bought the amazing changing station you just couldn't live without prior to the birth; you realise it's totally useless other than in the middle of the night as trekking up two flight of stairs with a poo covered baby during the day isn't much fun at all and actually a towel on the sofa or floor is so much more convenient. I still to this day think disposable change mats are a godsend. I keep them in a basket in the lounge with some wipes and a handful of nappies and you're good to go during the day every day.

Those first few days with baby are precious and full of uncertainty, so why not get a tip or two on how to make it just a little less scary and make it feel like you have someone holding your hand through it. My partner thought that by baby three, me wanting three cribs was madness as I should know what I'm doing by now, but now he is singing my praises. My only wish is that I had had the foresight to keep all the cribs and travel cots after each of the girls rather than recycling them believing we wouldn't use them again. Gosh how wrong was I...why we didn't just pop them in the loft I'll never know. This time I'm definitely keeping every last little item, much to my partner's distress or shall I say shock horror. At least it'll be there if we ever need it or friends wish to borrow it.

Back to my point, no-one wants to be sleep deprived and late for work lugging a crib downstairs at 6am, so why not make life easier if you can. Three sleeping areas does sound extravagant but let me explain, as it was actually an economy long-term and we doubled up on the uses of all of them.

In the end you'll find that by the time baby is two years old you would have bought all of these sleeping areas anyway; probably just not at once. So why not get all the use you can out of all of them and get the equipment in the beginning.

For Sophia our third daughter, upstairs in our bedroom we put the beautiful white cot that will see her through until about a year old. It's not in the nursery as she's not old enough to be in there on her own just yet, but why not use it now in your room rather than a moses basket? We didn't go for the cot bed this time though, as I've learnt from the other two that by the time they were about eighteen months old that they both wanted a proper bed not the pretty little baby bed I'd chosen.

Downstairs, yes I was a little greedy, but in the lounge we had a small crib. We used a crib not a moses basket as it's a little sturdier with other little faces peering over the sides and little fingers wanting to stroke their siblings' hair. I've found through experience that a crib lasts for longer as baby stays in it for around six months not just three. Either works well, just avoid the rocking ones as it never soothed any of our girls and you pay extra for this function, in addition to needing to show them from an early stage how to fall asleep in a bed not being coaxed to sleep. Babies really don't need any little tricks, as if they're tired they will sleep if the environment is right. The main reason I wanted a crib in the lounge with Sophia, is that's where we sit for coffee or in the evenings to relax.

The final cot, I had put in the room with all the kid's toys (where I spend far too much of my day). Believe it or not this is the last room to be decorated in our house too; it's as though the brightness of the toys lift it and bring a smile to your face without needing fancy wallpaper or in reality we just haven't got round to it and never imagined I would be in there so much. This is where I've had the travel cot assembled now so that Sophia can be involved all the time with the girls and yes she was in there all snug in her first few days home. She slept and her sisters played.

My view of it is why buy a travel cot just to visit friends and for long weekends? They've got so much more use than that. Whenever we go on a day out it comes with us as, invariably, friends' houses aren't entirely suitable for little ones and it's a comfortable familiar place for a nap or a safe play. Travel cots don't need to break the bank though, there are many good ones on the market that don't cost the earth but stop and think, will you actually use the vibrating mattress or lullaby functions? I still haven't on baby three, so all you really need is one that looks nice, is easy to put up and down and preferably has a bassinet in it so you can use it right from birth.

Why not get the cot and use it now in your room rather than it collecting dust in the nursery. Get a crib or moses basket in your most used room and splash out on the travel cot (or borrow one) in the beginning as everyone gets one eventually. You can then have them set up in the most convenient places for you, where you actually want baby to be, as the nursery won't get even one night's sleep out of it until baby is at least four months old. Why not decorate the nursery once you can actually see baby's personality coming through. Rather than babyish themes, make sure it's easy to adapt and change by the age of two, six etc. Harriett our eldest is long past butterflies and at the age of five is now into pirates so the stripy wallpaper rather than floral really was an investment! Focus on the more important aspects before baby arrives rather than wall colour as this can be sorted out anytime but the right cot, mattress and car seat really can't wait.

Mattresses for babies are a minefield, but remember all are fine as long as they meet safety standards and are new for each child. The ones with the zip off top layers that are available are really worth having if you can, as they can be washed and refreshed so easily making those sick and poo accidents much much easier to clean up.

The best investment when it comes to sleeping arrangements is sheets and all the bedding accessories. I can't stress this enough and there are only a few exceptions to this like cot bumpers. After three children I still don't see the need for them. Once you have finally chosen your cot and been through the mammoth task of getting it home and building it along with the mattress regardless of if the top layer zips off or not, get a mattress protector too. Trust me on this, the extra £15 spent on this protector will be invaluable when baby has a tummy bug and is sick and this will definitely happen as children don't just vomit once in the night. I've been in the situation where we've been through every sheet in the house and had the Detol out scrubbing the mattress clean at 2am, which isn't much fun I can tell you so invest wisely now! Look into brushed cotton, Egyptian cotton etc. If you're going to spend money anywhere it should be on what baby will use most…bed.

That's the basics now onto the actual bedding. I've got little to say about cot bumpers and baby duvets or coverlets, as I've already mentioned, other than yes they're pretty, but I find them really pointless. I didn't buy any this time as I find it's just one more thing to wash in my mind, as babies wriggle and so rarely stay under them. They tend to be too warm as well, so that's why the sheets are so so critical.

On top of the mattress and mattress protector place a fitted sheet. These can be cold to lay baby on in those winter months, so at the foot end place a blanket ready to tuck baby in, but pulled back so you don't have to do it with baby in your arms and at the head end of the cot cover the mattress with another small jersey sheet. This has two uses, one it's warmer against baby's face than a standard sheet and the other is when baby dribbles their milk you only need to wash and change a tiny sheet not one that takes up half the washing machine. So that's a full size sheet covering the entire mattress protector, a small sheet covering the head end of the cot and a blanket covering the foot end of the cot.

Making up beds like this for baby makes life that little more simple, but ensure you have enough for at least two changes though or you'll get caught out one night like we did with the never ending vomit. The reason I say this is babies are sick, not in the sense we know as adults but often through just taking on too much milk and my experience is babies don't just do this once in the night but can happen two or three times and you don't want to be scrubbing a mattress in the middle of the night like me, or to run out of sheets. If you catch the little accidents quick enough, then you can just whip the top sheet off by the head and job done. Predominantly it just protects the main bedding from those little dribbles and will save you a lot of washing in the long run and the crib sheets can be used at the head end on all toddler beds, making dribble nights easy and giving all those small sheets extra functionality.

Gosh I didn't think I had so much to say on beds but my life would just be spent up and down the stairs and washing if I didn't have the cots strategically placed around the house or carefully planned bedding.

Day 1 – The showering debacle

The other mind boggler in the first few days, is when baby wakes and you want a shower do you really want your beautiful newborn being left out of sight? In our case with the dog too; we trust our dog implicitly but you really never do know an animal so take no chances. What do you do, stay in your pajamas all day? Not shower? It's difficult, so how I overcame this was with a baby swing. It is a simple rocking chair suitable from birth with a few flashing lights on it to give the baby something to look at and soon we had formed our morning routine. I got up when the alarm went off, which invariably woke Sophia up, but this was fine. I got her a fresh bum, dressed her and popped her into the swing for a ten minute play whilst I had a shower and got myself ready.

The swing came into every room with me when she was little, including the bathroom. You can do this with a newborn too as long as the swing or bouncer is suitable from birth and gives enough support. Make the day work for you by not allowing the baby to dictate from day one how the family functions.

Occasionally Sophia cried in the swing when she was a bit older and I was taking a little too long for her liking, but as I could see her the entire time, I knew she was fine and that there was no need for me to rush and there we have it;

our routine for the first few months was born. It is knowing little things like this, that remove the first panicky ways of doing every day things. Baby can come with you albeit not always in your arms.

Predominantly people are completely misled into thinking they have to be holding baby all the time or be comforting them or rocking them. It really isn't necessary, would you like all that fuss? Try if you can to give baby a little of their own time and space it's healthy and it is okay for them to lie in their crib or under the play arch without you constantly fussing.

The same is true of cooking; you can still do it, as baby really doesn't need to be your arms at all times. Try and create somewhere where baby can be seen by you and you can see baby when you're cooking and then you'll find you won't rush or panic as that's how accidents happen. When you can always see your little darling, things seem to go at a much more leisurely pace surrounded by an aura of calm rather than haste and clumsiness; allowing your day to run a little smoother.

The first few weeks we are all lulled into a false sense of security. Baby wakes, feeds then sleeps and we think 'not bad, I can do this'. It's a simple pattern and a very easy routine but gradually they're awake for longer between sleeps and feeds. Remember though that they don't need to be constantly entertained and just watching you do the dusting or washing up is fascinating to them.

Sophia is thirteen weeks now and can easily stay awake for four hours at a time, so don't wait for baby to sleep before getting on with your day as you'll never get anything done or go anywhere! With our first born, I was the jumpy Mum attending to every cry, whimper and movement, always picking her up and trying to soothe her but now I realise that was about what I needed not what she needed so be careful.

Ask yourself every time your baby makes a noise is it doing them any harm? In all cases the answer is 'no'. If you know baby is well fed, burped, changed, and tired through play, why shouldn't they lie in their crib and have a little chat to themselves or even at first cry themselves to sleep? None of our girls have lasted more than ten minutes without dropping to sleep unless they genuinely needed an extra nappy change or something similar. Even to this day it breaks my heart to hear them cry even for a moment but 99.9% of the time they don't need or even want me. It's just a sign of frustration or tiredness or even dreaming. When playing, Sophia regularly cries or has a little moan; this is only because she can't do something or can't get something that she wants. Me doing it all for her is what my heart screams, but my head knows it won't do her any good. She needs to push herself to reach the ball to advance her abilities rather than me doing it for her. I want my children to try, not to expect it all to be done for them.

What I did learn by baby three about tiredness and sleep disturbances though, was that by me checking them I was actually the cause of their waking and as long as I could see them then why shouldn't they settle themselves? This time I have gone to the extreme though and Sophia doesn't require any bedtime comfort at all as she has never come to expect it. When she is tired she has her bottle then, when dozy, she is put into her bed to settle herself and so far this only takes seconds. My elder girls both liked to be fed lying down as babies and sleep-deprived me did, on occasion, fall asleep feeding them in my arms when I was breast feeding and I still beat myself up over this to this day, as it's so so dangerous. As soon as the girls were on the bottle I stopped picking them up in the night all together because I just couldn't risk falling asleep, and instead, I just put my arm through the bars of their cot with the bottle to feed them at 4am when they woke thirsty. This time the routine has been the same from the outset.

From birth through to about four months no matter how the day had been, I woke Sophia up at 9pm or by the latest 9.30pm and changed her nappy and gave her a small feed then bed it was for her. With the 4am feed though, even from birth I have never picked her up. I've just rolled over, put my hand through the bars with the bottle and fed her that way. Within ten minutes (and never more than that) she's fast asleep and this is purely because she doesn't associate that midnight feed with comfort, it's purely for fluids. Now at thirteen weeks though its nappy change at 8pm, bed then hello 6am so that is fantastic for me and if we get a quirky night then its only…lean over for ten minutes at 4am, so it is not totally exhausting. We all learn our own way, but ask yourself why are you picking your baby up? Is it for you? Is it for baby? Why not express the night feed and take it in turns with your partner?

If you can express, it does open an entire new world of independence for you as a Mum. It allows you to have an hour away from baby without feeling guilty and you can share the night feed when you're so tired you don't think you'll ever wake up. Why can't Grandma feed baby whilst you have a long bath? Why can't Dad feed baby whilst you take the dog for a walk? Why can't Dad feed baby on a Saturday night when there's no work in the morning. We're not talking about you abandoning your newborn with a stranger but an hour or two with a trusted someone even with you in the house; it is still good for you and your baby's independence to not totally be reliant on you.

If you're with baby 24/7 and do all the feeds, all the changes all the baths, all the settling then you won't enjoy your time with baby and it'll seem like even more hard work than it really is. Your baby should be a joy and an hour away will let you enjoy baby all over again and again, and you'll appreciate all those precious moments all the more because you'll have some space and time to be with just you rather than being just Mum constantly. A little space brings a fresh perspective and outlook on virtually all situations and for me is nearly as good as an extra twelve hours sleep.

Sleep or exhaustion?

The bit no-one ever talks about with any truth surrounding it is sleep. No professional or friend for that matter will tell you that you don't just wake up tired one day. After the exhaustion of giving birth you never quite recover. You use up all your energies in nurturing baby for nine months, then actually being in labour and then you want to spend every minute you can with your newborn, when what you really need is sleep. It won't seem like it but the reality is that after giving birth you will and do need sleep. At this point most think 'this isn't too bad, I can do this' and then the adrenalin and excitement take over and there's a huge surge of new energy that comes with a newborn baby and it seems like a great idea to see all your friends and family when you're only just adjusting to being woken up every two or three hours.

Everyone wants to show off their newborn, it's only natural and for a few days you feel like super woman that you can do it all. I even gave my partner a lie in the day after Sophia was born I was that energised; but stop and take stock. This behavior is madness and this will all catch up eventually and after night after night of disturbed sleep are you really still going to be that patient with everyone and be able to keep up with the washing?

Everyone says sleep when baby does, but life goes on and that doesn't really happen especially when it's baby two or three. No-one tells you that just as you go into a deep sleep, this is when the door goes, the phone rings or baby wakes for an unexpected feed. You never actually catch up on the sleep; you just learn to live comfortably on less. It's like being drip fed over months and years sleep deprivation. I'd love to be able to stay in bed till 11am but now my body clock says good morning at 6am every day regardless. This is when the girls naturally wake too, as they say 'early to bed early to rise' and actually I like having my evenings with my partner and he's up to go to work early too so this suits us and is in tune with the girls natural rhythms'. It's just not the time I would get up if I had a choice but it's the only way to realistically manage our family's days and meet all our commitments.

The only way life goes on comfortably, is by taking it in turns with a baby. We worked out early on that in any relationship with children the most common row has to be who is the most tired; well in our house at least. Who is more exhausted because of work, looking after the kids, doing the chores, who got up to get the beaker of water in the night. Well reality is you are as tired as each other, so the one and only time you can have a lie-in is at the weekend so decide before a glass of wine who will have a small lie-in on a Saturday and who will have one on the Sunday. It's not a lie-in that a student would approve of, but when you're up at 6am every day then a 9am cuddle from a four year old is a lovely way to be woken up especially when all they want is for you to play.

Make each other a coffee and make the weekends fair, well as fair as you can. What is the point of you both having your eyes out on stalks? Children are exhausting on every level from a newborn to toddler to teenager and you never recover the sleep not truly and if you're that exhausted, how are you finding the time to spend three hours a night on social networking sites? I know I haven't. So be sensible and go to bed at a reasonable hour. There have been many occasions when I've been in bed by 8.30pm and been so so pleased to have my head on the pillow.

Baby Holding

All Grandparents will hate this element of the manual but when you bring your newborn home, of course you want to show them off but all the visitors could actually do more harm than good. If someone has a cold do not feel bad by saying 'no' to them holding the baby or if you know they smoke then get them to use antibacterial gel on their hands first, but most importantly don't do like many do and just pass the baby around. The poor little thing has just been thrust into the world and only knows Mum because of milk at the moment. Let yourself and your partner bond with baby before all and sundry try and hold baby. Can you imagine how unsettling it must be to be in a room not knowing who anyone is when you can only see about 5cm in front of your face? Let little one settle in and be vocal in saying 'no'. This is your baby and you shouldn't be intimidated into letting other people do what they like.

Babies fool you into a false sense of security as, to begin with, when you've got your burst of energy they only eat and sleep so you think 'this is easy I can do this'. Then it all changes but remember fresh air, exercise and seeing people fix most issues for a new Mum. You notice that every time you go to the beach you get a sleepy feeling; it's the fresh air and the same works for children. Fresh air exhausts them but for a newborn there is so much to see that they've never seen before that makes it all the more tiring. Imagine never seeing a cloud before or a bird or the trees swaying in the wind or the smell of the sea. It will be like discovering them all over again, but together. All these experiences we take for granted, but enjoy them with your baby. Make time every week if not every day to go out for a walk, it'll be good for your waistline too. We've got a dog so I really have no excuse to not get out there in the fresh air.

Introduce baby to new things everyday and find a baby group as soon as you can. What you'll find is there's always someone there having a more difficult time than you and soon you'll come away feeling refreshed just from realising not everyone has it figured out. You've spent time with grown-ups, baby has had a roll around and heard new voices and it's a change of scenery away from the house. Try a few groups though until you find one you like; they're definitely not all the same.

Bath time

From a holding baby perspective, as you've already found out now you're home, you must always support baby's head until they can do this by themselves at around three to four months, but there really is nothing nicer than cradling a little one in the nook of your arm having a sneaky cuddle and when they're fresh from the bath all snug and sleepy with that fabulous new baby smell. In my experience babies have very sensitive skin so just be wary of what you wash baby in those first few times, as some of the well known brands have brought my girls up red and blotchy. Look for gentle and organic if so inclined and natural ingredients for your newborns delicate skin.

Bath time is a real minefield for a new parent; how do you hold baby? How do you get them in and out of the bath? How do you actually get the towel on them? What temperature should the water be? Well the answer to this is to get your baby a bath; you only use it for a month or so, so don't break the bank on this one. Get a foam insert, small sponge, flannel, thermometer and towel ready. You can get these as small gift sets too (great for the baby list). Once all the bath bits are ready ensure you have the sleep suit, vest and nappy waiting on the change mat. Put baby in their cot whilst you prepare the bath as it is impossible with them in your arms or just outright dangerous with glass shower screens and hot water.

Put the baby bath in your bath with all your bits and put the towel flat on the toilet seat…yes the toilet seat! It is not the most idyllic place but is the floor any better? This is a family bathroom the answer is 'no'; it was all cleaned at the same time! Turn your hot tap on and the cold at the same time and fill the baby bath to about two inches below the rim. At this point check the baby bath thermometer and adjust the temperature so it's perfect for baby but to you and me it will feel a little colder than we're used to. Make sure the foam pad and flannels etc are the same temperature too by ensuring they are completely immersed in the water too. Now go and get baby and get them undressed and yes there will be a couple of little shivers to tug at your heart strings when baby is only a week or two old but it is just the change of temperature on their skin and it's only for a second or two.

Here goes... feet first, gently lay baby on the foam insert in the baby bath, ensuring the head obviously is above the water. Now you will notice you have two hands free to gently adjust baby and wash their beautifully soft hair and every little chubby crease under their chins and arms, as they are perfectly nestled on the foam. Hygiene wise though make sure you use one sponge exclusively for washing the body and bum etc and a flannel specifically for the face.

Baby won't need long in the bath at this point, but you can gradually extend it into play time. In our case its wind down time ready for bed, so no toys just bubbles from the girls wash which doubles up as a bath foam and it's more than enough to amuse them and use up that last and final ounce of energy. It works for me too after a long day!! Once baby is washed you'll soon realise that you don't have three hands, so how on earth are you going to manage to get them out, but follow these simple steps and you'll be well away.

Firstly I'd always use a hooded towel for a newborn, but any bath towel works for babies after about six months as they've grown out of those pretty baby ones by that point. Again invest in the fancy towels when they are a little older and then they will last a year or two but at this stage think functional. A £6 towel will do as well as the £25 with the embroidery and the saving can be spent on other essentials. Anyway I side lined. Back to getting baby out of the bath; place one hand under baby's neck and the other under their bum so fully supported and lift straight up and immediately lay baby as though placing them in their cot on the towel. Take one hand from under baby and place on their tummy and then with the other fold the towel over one way and then swap hands on the tummy and fold over the other side as though wrapping baby up in a blanket. Tuck babies head into the hood so they're totally cosy then one hand under their bum and one under their neck and lift to place baby up on your shoulder and carry them off to get dried immediately. Don't hang about at this stage as babies get cold very quickly, so make sure you have everything ready first.

I find that rubbing some oil into their skin after a bath relaxes the muscles and saves using a lotion too, but again apply it quickly and only do one leg at a time and so on keeping the rest of baby bundled up and warm. Then put on the nappy, vest and sleep suit ready for a bottle and bed as the routine goes in our house. The only thing I have really learnt about babies is actually, it doesn't matter what time you bath them, early morning, lunchtime or bed time but what does matter is ensuring its always the same, so baby knows what to expect. It's about routine, the same length of time (or as close to) the same views to see, the same smells, same order of washing such as hair always last. You'll thank me for this order in the long run even if it does seem a little OCD to begin with. If it's different every time how can baby begin to relax?

Muslin cloths

Moving back to practicalities, what is the big attraction with these so called muslin cloths I hear you ask and to a non-parent they seem utterly pointless but to those with a baby you know they are precious, they're a god send, and they're invaluable.

Just wait, you'll see and feel the mess under chins when baby has their milk and it's dribbling all down your arm not to mention how useful they are in clearing u,p those little or not so little sick moments.

Consider this purchase again though. You'll need about ten realistically unless you want to be constantly washing and get coloured ones where possible. Can you really keep the white ones white? Also you'll find your washing machine has never had so much use as it will now baby's here. Check to see if it has a quick wash function and a hand wash function if you're lucky. It will ensure you get the best use out of those gorgeous hand knitted cardigans and hats and booties and those precious snuggly things they attach themselves to. No-one really has time to do it by hand and you'll get so much more use out of the clothes, and even more so, if you drape a muslin under baby's chin when feeding and on your shoulder when comforting baby. You'll be surprised how few people will tell you when there's sick on your shoulder!

PART TWO
The Everyday Reality

Fitting it all in

Predominantly the key to not losing your mind or personality is organisation and routine. Since having the girls I've got a memory like a sieve so, for me, I need a diary and I do check this daily alongside my very laughable never-ending lists. For me this is the only way I get it all done. I have lists for everything from the weekly food shopping to DIY that needs doing in the house and I use these to prioritise my time. There are things that need doing daily, like the school run so I know exactly how much time I have (which isn't a lot) for other things. To squeeze in the cleaning, for example, I've split the house into seven zones and tackle a different area every day on top of vacuuming downstairs every day and this ensures I get the most time with the girls and it's always done. It doesn't take long when it's split up whereas one big clean is exhausting.

At the moment Sophia sits in her swing and watches me and the older two love to grab a duster and pretend to be Mummy, thinking they're all grown up and it helps me with the skirting boards too. It doesn't need to be a chore for the girls when I'm cleaning, and when they don't want to join in, this is ample time for dot to dot or to get some practice on those spellings that they never really get round to. As I manage to get most of it done during the day, it enables my partner to return from work and enjoy quality time with the girls and I don't have to be that crazy woman cleaning at 10 o'clock at night.

I will be honest here though, as I have had some help with this recently. Our commitments have increased and my partner's office hours have drastically increased (as well as the stress levels) so I have taken on more of the social aspects of our family, such as attending all the school assemblies when the girls are on stage, rather than taking it in turns and attending all the birthday parties they get invited to and so on. In order for me to do all of this, we had to compromise and so, we have enlisted the help of a cleaner. This means I can take the extra load and allow my partner to commit more heavily to his work role.

We re-prioritised to ensure we weren't compromising the things that really mattered to the girls, but we didn't get the help until Harriett was nearly five, so we really did do it all whilst working full time for a very long time on our own. Splitting it all out and the girls helping was the only way to get it all done. Don't misunderstand me here; I'm by far a lady of leisure. I still clean the bathrooms and vacuum every day, as well as the constant washing and dishwasher loads, I just have a couple of hours help every week now to ensure things like the picture rails are dusted (my view is, if you can't see it, leave it till last!).

Scheduling the house like this has also aided our household routine, as by the time Daddy's home, it's that final burst of energy from the girls to expel (often in the garden) and then it's book time. This special time is something we've always cherished as a family since they were old enough to sit on our knees unsupported. This lovely family time leads quietly on to bedtime which starts at 7.30 pm in our house and then thirty minute intervals for each, but we do ensure we take it in turns between us so it's not always Mummy or Daddy putting one to bed. This way each of the girls get some quality time with us and have their own bedtime which does make it a little smoother and quieter. The added bonus is, us having our own time. It's the only way a relationship really survives I think. You do need time on your own together even if it's just making supper, do it together and maybe join each other for a glass of wine and sneak a little cuddle in there too, even if it is just by the cooker. It's not long it's just the two of you every day, so make it worth every second. This is all the more critical for households with two working parents.

Make time to be there for each other, no matter how small the gesture may seem. Sometimes my partner just switching the oven on to bring it up to temperature brings a tear to my eye. Not because I'm the weepy soft sort, but because he doesn't need to and it becomes one less thing for me to do. It is thoughtful consideration that makes a difference to me not how many times I'm brought flowers.

Childcare and working the myth

Everyone has an opinion on childcare and working when you're pregnant. My only view is to go with your instinct. Some people have no choice and in order to sustain the household then Mum needs to work, but there are also the cases where Mum chooses to work or stay at home. Maternity rights and benefits are numerous these days and there is so much bumpf around on this that I'm not even going to touch upon it but I just want to let you know, how over the years, our choices have changed and what has worked for us overtime.

With our firstborn Harriett, it never occurred to me not to work and I couldn't bear the thought of baby groups and coffee mornings. I had studied and worked for years to start achieving my goals and I didn't see why a family should change the direction of my ambition. However I faced a quite substantial amount of negativity about it from family, but we stuck to our guns, although it was conditional. We made the decision about this like everything else, together. We said I would only work if we had the right childcare and the moment that was compromised I would stay at home. To us both, we felt that was more than fair and enabled me

31

to have the best of both worlds; motherhood and be the career girl. Well, we found a fabulous nursery that worked with my routine and I didn't have a single concern or worry about Harriett going there; the carers were lovely and the other children were gorgeous and it was so good for her independence and social skills, even at six months old.

Predominantly though, it was good for her to learn that Mummy always comes back and that her needs are met, even when I wasn't there and the same was true with our second born Lily and she attended the same nursery too. It was only when we were looking at the finances of having two in nursery full time, that we realised that a Nanny was a cheaper option and they would come to our house, look after the children in their own environment. If I didn't have time to get them dressed or breakfasted; as happens to all of us some mornings, then it didn't matter as the Nanny could step in and the bonus was, she made their food and did their washing too.

For us this resulted in combined care though as the girls loved their nursery. We had a Nanny for a few days and nursery for a few days. I thought we had the best of both worlds again; I was enjoying my job and the people, the girls were happy and our Nanny was fantastic. I got the good fun time with the girls with little to no tantrums in the evenings and we were balancing the weekend lie-ins between us and sharing most of the chores. It was a little too good to be true to be honest and then our world changed overnight. Our Nanny could no longer do the days we needed and the nursery couldn't have them any more days. We were devastated, but I did the right thing for the girls; I left my job.

My world was shattered at the time, but little did I know, it was the best thing that could have ever happened to our family. The girls had a fabulous weekly routine already established, thanks to our Nanny, and I chose not to disturb it and I put on a brave face and went to the toddler groups that the girls already knew and the library story mornings and you know what, I really enjoyed them in the end. I wasn't ready to be a stay at home Mum when we had Harriett and we couldn't afford it either, but with Lily I'd really settled into motherhood.

It's not all talk of babies when you are out as a Mum like people think. It can be if you want, but it is what you make it and as Mums we regularly talk world politics, finance, philosophy, psychology and law. Everyone has their own knowledge base and it's fascinating to share it, even over a bad cup of coffee and slightly stale biscuit. Get out there, try a few groups, you may even make a friend or two with like minded people like I have, but most of all a change of scenery just stops you going crazy and the kids always have fun regardless of what the adults are like.

You have probably guessed by now that we did look for alternative childcare for many months, but we were spoiled by what we had and nothing else seemed to measure up and so I stayed at home and with baby three and that is still the plan. However she will be going to a nursery or a Nanny one day a week, as it was such a rewarding experience for Harriett and Lily. The hard bit is finding one again. I have a lot to thank the nursery and Nanny for in terms of our girls' behavior as it's prevented them from being clingy, enabling their confidence to grow naturally aiding their social skills and ensuring manners are always present. I really do feel this was one of the most rewarding experiences for our family unit as a whole.

Arguments

When there's a new baby in the house, it's the most magical yet stressful time you'll ever encounter. The pressures as a couple are immense even before work re-commences and many don't survive this mammoth test. Together you're battling sky high hormones, exhaustion and change in lives so dramatic it's impossible to turn back and re-create what once was. You're facing uncertainty, confusion, feelings of inadequacy just to start, so it's hardly surprising not all relationships make it through these times. For those that do find a way to muddle through, it is with compromise and understanding each other in a way they never knew they could, but this happy equilibrium will only come with row after row!

To this day, I don't know a single couple that has made it without experiencing the biggest arguments of their lives. Those that do survive don't hold on to the anger and they remember that it's exhaustion impairing things and magnifying the smallest of issues. Does it really matter that the dishes were left overnight? or that you got up one more time in the night with the baby than your partner? It is hard without question but do think and stop for a moment when you're bubbling towards that explosive row; where is baby? Can they hear? Can they see it happening? Children are so sensitive and do not underestimate what they pick up on or what they understand at any age. You wouldn't let a ten year old hear or see you arguing, so why feel its okay for your newborn?

Try and get through the hard times as best you can as there will be numerous occasions, but try and remember how strong you are all together and, in the grand scheme of things is this particular argument really that important or is it just an overly emotionally heightened situation? Remember baby and do what is right for your beautiful family unit and that unit will only stay strong and together if that's what you really want it to be.

Cost

As everyone knows having a baby is expensive. It adds up quickly, so use those baby gift lists to keep track of purchases and once the essentials are covered off then get the cute teddies and gorgeous outfits if you can then afford it. Most of all take complete advantage of the sales. Armed with your baby list (yes we all have them…the wish list) and knowing the date of baby's arrival you can pick up clothes months in advance at a huge discount. Buy for the following season and stock up on those essential, baby-grows, t-shirts and hats, but definitely wait for the sales for the big purchases. Not forgetting my favorite; online discounts and vouchers that come with the baby magazines.

There are lots of savings to be had out there so keep an eye out, save all those vouchers and sign up online to all the baby web sites and to the baby stores online and you'll be awash with offers seasonally, in excess of what you'll ever need, from clothes to toys, furniture, food and nappies. If you have space, then buy in bulk and wait for the supermarkets baby promotions and you'll never pay full price for a nappy or for your baby products online again.

This is another contentious area, nappies; do you go with disposable or reusable? Actually, these days convenience wise there isn't a vast difference. Just make sure you really do have time for all the washing if using reusables because as a working Mum I knew I didn't have the time or inclination but I definitely did consider it this time. However we decided I have enough washing to do already with three girls, without a couple of extra loads every week but if you're a home Mum I'd seriously consider it.

We rarely paid full price for Lily and Sophia's things after learning from how much we spent with Harriett. We saved nearly 40% on our last pushchair. Okay we bought it six months early, but we saved a fortune. It's your money, don't give it away, you earned it.

My biggest tip to friends to ensure funds really aren't wasted, not only by you but family, is to always make sure the children get exactly what they want for Christmas, birthdays and yes Easter too. Don't be too shy to tell people that they don't actually want the plastic dolly, but have their heart set on a bunny. It saves disappointment and people wasting their money, but mostly manages people's expectations around the children. For example at Easter, as the girls are all young, they get a small packet of chocolate buttons each and from family they receive pocket money toys. It's so much more fun and you're not still stuck with twenty eggs come next Christmas! Harriett got a kaleidoscope this year and Lily fairy snap. It doesn't need to be big presents, but just fun gifts. Tell people in advance, as you'll be surprised how many eager relatives buy mountains of chocolate for a one year old, so start how you mean to go on.

The same applies at Christmas, we had six advent calendars on Harriett's second Christmas and she was only eighteen months old then. People don't seem to realise that children and definitely babies really don't need that much chocolate; if any. To combat this over indulgence in chocolate, especially at Christmas, we've got a fabric re-fillable advent calendar for the girls and we tuck in bouncy balls and colouring pencils and the odd chocolate. The year in question, we suffered for weeks after Christmas as we had so much chocolate given to us and Harriett didn't understand why she couldn't have chocolate every day after

Christmas anymore. It's just too much of a minefield of tantrums for me, so we stopped it. No it's not cruel, it's being thoughtful.

Christmas is the season of joy, but we learned fast that our girls are spoiled by everyone around them and have been given so much in such a short space of time. Now we've tried to guide friends and family away from gifts and more towards creating memories instead. The toys are soon forgotten and end up in the pile with the others but Harriett's first red bus journey to London Zoo with her God Father, will stay with her forever. A morning swimming followed by lunch on their own without their siblings means so much more to a child. All children go out and about and on special trips, but focused attention individually is so so precious and the smile in return beats a thousand moments of tearing off wrapping paper. Apart from their utter enjoyment, it gives us as parents a sneaky break too. You'll be surprised at the change in dynamics when you have one sibling less for a few hours.

Presents and chocolate really don't hurt, but do ensure it's in moderation and that the toys are what the children really enjoy. Harriett's worst nightmare would be a dolly, but you wouldn't know that without asking me and the same goes for the fact that she doesn't like jelly sweets, but loves boiled ones. No-one wants to be or appear ungrateful when receiving gifts, but children are excessively honest and if you don't tell someone then the children will do it for you; so save the embarrassment and talk about it long before Christmas and birthdays come about.

PART THREE
The Oh So Needed Practicalities With Baby

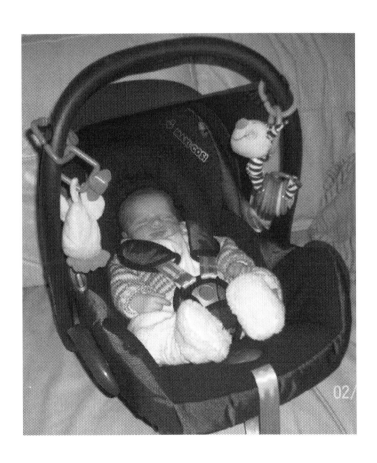

Pushchairs and Car seats

Pushchairs and car seats I've found is the area of greatest expense for new parents. Ask your friends for advice here regarding what they find works and what didn't for their family. Over the years I've had loads of pushchairs and there is only two I would buy again. The first is the Mamas and Papas Pilko3; it's from a pram to a pushchair, huge basket, easy to fit rain cover, hood that doubles as a sun canopy, light weight, folds small. It's durable, has a back step for older children two handles rather than a bar so I can load all the shopping bags on when the basket's full and it looks quite nice too. No I'm not endorsing it, it just really works well for me and that's why. The second pushchair I loved was the Ziko stroller which was light, compact, so easy to maneuver but very sturdy.

Think about your pushchair before you venture to the shops with your partner too. This is days and days worth of research to ensure you get the right one and we've been through five so far, so I'm starting to become a pushchair geek. Simple things are worth considering, like I wanted a back step for the tired little ones. I know from experience you only use the carry cot function for about three months, so this wasn't a priority for me even though they look so cute. On average you end up spending hundreds of pounds more than you need to on an accessory or function you'll rarely use in the long run, is three months of use worth the extra money? The drop in car seat function, I only use for about three weeks and they're heavier so does it make a difference to you? It did to me; with carrying two girls, two school bags, two PE bags, opening doors and carrying a baby seat, as you can imagine is a talent in itself; but anything that lightens an already heavy load is welcome in my world. So I focused on the rest of the pushchair's functionality rather than prettiness; like the size of the under basket, maneuverability, having two handles for hanging the shopping on etc.

We've had every kind of pushchair at one time or another, it seems, including a double one and an all terrain pushchair at one time too. It was fabulous but when walking the dog I always tended to use the baby sling (and for doing chores in the house) and so the all terrain one was only really used around the shops and occasionally cobbles so again be sensible and think of your lifestyle. Is the extra outlay really for a purpose? Forget the gorgeous accessories; can you clean it in an hour not twenty four when baby's been sick? Will it take the shopping? How much mud will the wheels collect, as who wants that in their car? Will it actually fit in the car? Is it comfy and roomy for a toddler? Does it lie flat for sleeping? Can you put it up and down one handed whilst holding baby? If you don't consider these angles, you really will regret it once all that money's been spent and you go home with the wrong one!

The carry cot is cute and it comes in nice pretty colours but will you genuinely use it? Cost it out…how much will it equate to per outing? Oh and remember, you're not the only one to push baby so would Dad or Granddad be embarrassed by the shocking pink floral pushchair or not? Will you use the change bag it comes with or would you prefer an everyday bag that meets all your needs? Are the liners cosy enough? Forget the sun canopy; we've had all of them and we always resort to dropping a muslin or blanket down from the hood when required, as the others are never at the right angle or are just too flimsy. Most importantly, how easy is it to clean when baby's sicked an entire bottle of milk over it? Oh yes, I've been there many a time, and it only happens when you're in a rush and baby has to go back into it, so take time over this decision as the right pushchair should see you through from newborn until they're walking all the time (about 2-3 years old).

So think about what you want from a pushchair, as for me they all differ immensely, especially when you have to clean them when baby's been sick. Can the straps go in the washing machine for example? Can you push it whilst comforting baby in your arms? How robust are the wheels? How long will you actually use the carry cot function for? Where will the change bag go? Can you have a drink to hand? Cup holders were a big thing for me. I like my coffee in the morning. Make this a very practical decision. There's a lot of good stuff out there, just don't purchase a pushchair because it purely looks nice, it's a huge amount of money to just waste.

Car seats are another whole minefield though. Use your money wisely here too, as with three children I required a very light-weight seat which ruled out all travel systems for us, as an extra pound in weight is a lot when you're carrying baby in it. We also required easy to fit seats as putting three kids in the car in the rain is miserable when you're then fiddling with a seat belt, so it was Isofix for us. The bulk in the seat also played a factor as not all cars can take a baby seat, toddler seat and booster across the back without them being very specific ones, so there was lots of measuring and research done by us, well really me to ensure all our requirements were met, including can I see over the seats when I'm driving. No joke, one toddler seat was so high it meant I could barely use my rear view mirror.

Also consider how easy is it to clean with a sicky baby; can all of the cover and straps go in the washing machine or is it wipe clean only? And how easy is it to move between vehicles when Grandparents want to give you a break for example. The colour and pattern of the pushchairs and car seats really are the least of your worries.

I've found the best way to start is forget the price, find all that meet your criteria and then narrow it down from there. These purchases are used daily, for years, so definitely spend a little more here. It's not the area to scrimp and save on considering the time they spend in them, so comfort is key. Don't forget the sun blinds or black out windows for the car, as babies can still get sun burnt in winter in the car. Pushchair sun blinds and canopies aren't essential though as they're never quite in the right place so with factor 50, a hat and draped muslin or blanket over the hood you'll be fine.

Safety

Everyone is mad on home safety these days from in the car, to in the home. Don't rush out and buy everything when you're pregnant though, as this money is definitely better off in your bank account for now. Baby won't be up and about until around six months so invest in socket covers and cord winders when baby starts rolling and crawling. Other items, I'd assess at the time if you need them, as we didn't need cupboard locks with Harriett, but we definitely did with Lily. She was into everything, and being so active, pressure fit gates didn't contain her and soon our open plan home was more like a prison.

We'll see how Sophia goes, but I'm not worried, they're different in so many ways. As long as you remember that you don't use these items for long, as soon they will be confident enough to move around the house safely. The only item we really needed was the washing machine lock, as Lily regularly turned the hand washing onto a sixty degree boil wash drastically shrinking quite a few cashmere jumpers.

We take the safety of our girls incredibly seriously, but that doesn't equate to buying every gadget going. Children need to know their limitations and to be aware of household dangers and if everything's padded and out of reach how will they learn this? In addition, the danger is merely enhanced when going to friends' houses as the children will have no concept of what can or can't be touched and that a cupboard doesn't always need a lock on it, just saying 'no' should prevent it from being opened. It's not rocket science just common sense.

PART FOUR

The Bits We Never Thought
We Needed To Know

Sickness

The everyday in our home consists of eating, sleeping, school, work and sickness or as Harriett refers to it the 'lurgy'. With three girls under the age of five it seems that one of us is always sick with all the school and office germs making their way back home. Believe me I am far from being a medic and have no medical knowledge whatsoever but I have the experience of being a Mother with poorly children just like millions of other Mums out there and you get a feel for what is serious and what just needs a little Calpol and some TLC. Mainly it's just common sense.

Like most adults, all children are invariably sick from time to time and develop rashes and varying symptoms. Most are harmless and just the body's way of expelling a virus, but always check with a health professional if at all concerned. We often speak to our local pharmacist prior to booking a GP appointment, as I've gone rushing to the GP previously thinking the drowsiness, fever type symptoms were dramatic but in fact it was just teething.

I'd never ignore any symptoms, but children and babies regularly have fevers so know what's normal for your child and monitor their exact fluid intake throughout the duration of their illness. You'll find out over time that all the while they're eating and drinking they're not dehydrating, which is one of the biggest worries. Once you've given the obligatory Calpol or Nurofen check fever levels again and give ice cubes for kids to suck on or lollipops as they are a great way to bring down a temperature a little, as well as increasing their fluid intake slightly.

For our girls anything over 39 degrees was the time for me to start to worry, as naturally they sat towards the top end of 37 degrees and a big warning sign with our eldest

Harriett, was she would stop eating so this is the point I always sat up and paid close close attention. If poorly children perk up and can be distracted in new surroundings, then I've found there's often little to worry about even with a slight fever. Fevers come and go in most cases and go in peaks and troughs over time, so do monitor them over the duration.

Children will invariably only get sick out of doctors surgery hours and when you've got a Directors meeting at 8.30 am the following morning, so know where your nearest walk in centre is, but always call first as there may be a huge wait and a further five minute drive may be worthwhile to visit an alternative one or a late night pharmacy instead. Most of all don't panic. Stay calm, note temperatures, the time they were taken, every feed, fluid intake and the regularity of soiled and wet nappies along with the timings and dosage of any medicines given.

This does seem neurotic and my partner hates me doing this, but it's the details they ask you at the hospital if admission's required and they don't just ask you once. Often, if a GP can't determine the cause of the illness and there are high risk symptoms such as fever over 40 degrees or no wet nappies then monitoring takes place in the hospital to ensure nothing has been missed. It doesn't mean you should panic, just that the doctors are being cautious. So make sure you have your notes as they'll ask you every detail a thousand times over and at 2am you'll be thanking me and saying 'I told you so' to your partner as I did when Harriett got admitted with a fever.

Another note on illness is always take an overnight bag in the car if visiting the hospital and take snacks and drinks in with you, as once there it's not quick and it's difficult to leave the ward to get even a drink. In my case I had a clingy one year old terrified by all the lights, machinery and noises, so it was hard to even go to the bathroom. More often than not, if admitted it's an overnight monitoring of vitals such as temperature and blood pressure and discharge at 10am after doctors rounds with it all being something of nothing. Chances are all will be fine and you'll never need the notes, but that once in a blue moon when you do it's invaluable. So keep a small notebook handy or put the details in your phone.

Children and babies bounce back to normal as quickly as they got poorly and a blip will often have no explanation at all and with the three of them it feels like there's something at least once a month. If you've got a bad memory like me, then get a child health guide or familiarise yourself with symptoms online. Know what thrush looks like, what urine infection symptoms are, what post viral rash looks like, the symptoms of scarlet fever and chicken pox to name a few not forgetting conjunctivitis. Invest in a good digital ear thermometer and Calpol. In my change bag I keep a small medical kit with me at all times with Calpol sachets, aspirin for me, plasters for those little tumbles, antibacterial gel and a forehead thermometer for those just in case moments. As I've said before it only ever happens out of hours and away from home.

Bear in mind though doctors are only human and symptoms in children are very difficult to diagnose as children can't communicate the full picture of what's happening and how they're feeling, as they just don't have the vocabulary or experience. Only you know what's normal for your child and always seek advice if at all concerned or unsure of the symptoms.

Feeding

With the high levels of childhood sickness, boosting the immune system from the very beginning is the focus of most midwives and health visitors, as it's those early days of breastfeeding which give baby a head start. Rather than building their own stocks of anti-bodies they're receiving some of yours, however this leads to complete misery for some Mums. The pressures on breastfeeding are immense, especially from the health professionals that are there for you during your pregnancy.

It is a current hot topic to discuss breastfeeding baby for at least the first six months. There is little to no support for those of us that can't or only do so for a little while. Professionals shouldn't be making us feel like this. It's not their intention but the reality is you feel like a failure before you've really begun. The only thing that's important, is that if your choice is right for your family then it's the right choice. Bowing to the social pressure of feeding will only result in stress and strain both physically and emotionally. Try not to make any irrational decisions on this and of course change your mind at any point. Just ensure that this is a carefully considered and discussed decision. This is a very pressurised area and you're already doing the greatest and hardest job in the world loving and nourishing a baby with goodness, be it breast or bottle, the baby is still getting what it needs to thrive.

There are so many ways of making breastfeeding work for you though. I've got friends who feed in the day and express to do the night feed so partners can take a little of the strain every now and then. Then there are others that want to be a martyr and do every feed themselves; no-one gets a medal for this! And there are others like me that did a bit of everything; just breast with baby one then onto formula, breast and bottle with expressed milk then onto formula with baby two and then with little Sophia it was out of my hands and formula all the way. We can't predict how baby will take to feeding from any method or which formula they will take to. Unfortunately it's trial and error, as some brands are richer and heavier than others so consult with your health visitor and midwife if baby is being sick with any milk including breast, as they could have reflux or an intolerance.

Feeding is such a huge subject area which can be approached from so many angles but where to start? For me it's the moment you decide not to breastfeed anymore. Baby still needs milk, so equipment here is a big thing and invest wisely. Baby will be using these items for around a year and not all bottles are the same and not all babies get on with all of them so try one brand and if baby gets on with it stick with the bran. It will take a day or two for baby to get the hang of things and they will try and manipulate you into giving in and feeding them how they want to be fed, but persevere and be prepared to give it a few days.

You've made this decision because the current feeding method is no longer working for both you and baby; it is now one sided. When this happens it becomes unhealthy for you both as you'll resent it long term so go with your decision. For a newborn I would definitely recommend the half size bottles for the first couple of weeks as they're not as large and not as heavy on baby's mouth, but if you're putting an older baby of a few months onto bottles then by-pass these, as you'll only use them once or twice, so a waste of money overall. Go straight for the larger bottles and I made up the feed to the maximum amount i.e. 210mls water with 7 scoops of powder. Doing this kept the air out of the bottle and reduced the likelihood of colic as baby is getting all milk not air, allowing the natural pressure of the milk to determine a regular flow.

The brand doesn't particularly matter, but some milks are heavier than others and some babies struggle to keep them down but you can't predict this. Definitely get your midwife's advice on the brand and go with what they recommend. You just need to try one and see how baby gets. With Sophia it was milk number three that we tried that she liked. Oh what I did forget to say, was before baby is born keep one bottle and 1 litre of ready-made milk in the house, as you never know what is going to happen. Two of our girls fed straight away but with Sophia my milk didn't come in at all. I'd heard about this sometimes happening for women even though I wanted to breastfeed and so I kept some bits at home and good job too, as who wants to go to the shops hours after giving birth? Just precautionary but definitely a life saver, especially when you're tired and baby's hungry. I kept trying to feed Sophia, but she just got angry with me as she wasn't getting anything so we knew what we had to do. We had decided I'd give up breastfeeding by month three anyway.

I admire anyone who can feed for longer than three months, but I'm such a shy person and I find it difficult to feed with others around and find places I feel comfortable feeding when out. It's different for everyone and I've got friends that will feed anywhere and it makes life so much easier, but it's just not for me. This time though the decision was taken out of my hands and so our little angel had a bottle from the moment she arrived home. I did feel very judged though, as if I was depriving her but the fact is I wasn't; there was nothing to give her. Anyway it had nothing to do with anyone else other than our own little family. Don't listen to anyone on this, do what is right for your family and give up feeding when you're ready, not when you're told to. We can all only do our best. Once again though I got sidetracked into the detail of my own experiences; sorry…back to the rather important matter in hand, that cup of coffee and that biscuit!

Once you've chosen a bottle type and brand of milk, there's only a few more bits of kit that are essential to feeding. A steriliser is imperative, but stop and think for a minute. Is it compatible with your bottles and what is your lifestyle? When I was working we had a huge electric steriliser that felt like it did about a hundred bottles at once but it saved me so much time and I really couldn't have coped without it. Now I'm at home though, I decided sterilising two or three times a day didn't matter to me as I was home anyway, albeit in between errands and baby classes. We've got a small microwave one now and I haven't found one to be easier than the other, it's just a time difference and the quantity they hold.

Through the day my girls had about five bottles, then two at night and then the breakfast one, so it's a lot for a working parent to be dealing with and nurseries won't do this for you, however a Nanny will. Most definitely a childcare bonus! Again though, what will you do with the steriliser once you no longer need to sterilise the bottles, so don't spend silly money just make it functional to fit in with your life. It only has a few months use after all and the bottles are doubly sterilised if they go through the dishwasher in addition.

Alongside the big purchases, a big life saver for me has been milk portioners, so there's always milk in the change bag and ready to go and on the side for when baby wants it now and not in two minutes time as two minutes of screaming can feel like a lifetime. How's Dad or Grandma supposed to know the exact quantity when caught with no milk made up. I regularly made the milk up to the maximum amount as our girls liked the weight behind the milk to keep it flowing. They never drank the last 20ml or so as if they did they then ended up taking in too much air with it and so more in the bottle prevented this for us. Anyway it's all proportionate to the quantity of water to powder so maintain that. I've found that as long as ratios are maintained it's easier to make up a larger bottle, as every time the girls closed their eyes the bottle seemed to be nearly empty, which prompted a sudden alertness and outburst of crying so anything for any easy peaceful day!

So there you have it, feeding in a nutshell. There are a couple more short cuts though, such as baby drinking both readymade cartons and powdered formula as then you can just leave a carton in the car with a couple of nappies and wipes and you'll never get caught short. The other thing is, don't warm your baby's milk unless you feel you really can heat it every time, wherever you are.

I've seen it a hundred times; screaming baby that's been kept out too late and is hungry or got caught in a queue at the shops and then it's made to wait even longer whilst Mummy gets a stranger to warm the bottle in a restaurant or boil a kettle as baby knows no different and demands the bottle warming. Well what's wrong with room temperature? I'm not suggesting refrigerated just ask yourself why are you warming it? It's one more thing to do and worry about and at 3am no matter how much you love baby, for night ten in a row when you're exhausted, have you really got the energy? The cooled boiled water used to make the feeds is left out in a jug at room temperature before you heat it up again so why not use that? You can take a bottle of it with you, it's the same temperature as the cartons and it's less equipment, more accessible and generally just easier and quicker. It's not cruel not to warm the milk, it's not cold and to be honest it's not far off body temperature and my girls never having warm milk has saved me hours, saved tons of tantrums and lots of pointless equipment. You've got enough to carry already just being a Mum without a flask of boiled water too. Just think of the added weight in the change bag.

Weaning

That's milk dealt with, now onto a shorter section for me, weaning. Yes I did say shorter and that's because people generally over complicate this area and take the weaning books a little too seriously, after all they are just suggestions and guidelines. You know your child and when they're hungry the signs are clear and go with your instinct. For example you had a settled baby and now they push the bottle away… hello Mummy 'I'm hungry'. Fruit and vegetables are the way to start, first as a puree, then as a mash later on, then chunky by around eight months, but the fruit and vegetable stage is very important. If you do wean a little early like I did, then be sure to extend this stage as you don't want to encourage food intolerances and definitely not early childhood obesity; so keep within weaning food group guidelines. If baby is still hungry after having fruit or vegetables and weaning timelines have been met, then start to add in carbohydrate and protein. It worked for our girls, but I only introduced the protein in line with the recommended guidelines to ensure their bodies could process and digest all that I was giving them properly.

Lots of books tell you how to wean kids, but the focus for me here is the waste. Weaning baby takes a month or two not a lifetime, so what are you going to do with the twenty weaning pots or fancy machine that mushes the food for you. Be sensible here. Ice cube trays are a must; portion each item separately then you can mix and match the vegetables and meats depending on what you feel like. Don't do special baby dinners, just take a few carrots out of your roast or grab the avocado from the fruit bowl. Then it won't feel like such a chore, as eventually baby will eat what you eat anyway and you don't want to develop fussy habits.

Try the widest variety of fruit and vegetables that you can. My girls adore grapes but equally mango too and don't be afraid to try baby on foods you don't like either. I've finally given in to having bananas in the house and peeling them, but I still can't bring myself to have a bite when the girls want to share. Just because I don't like a food certainly does not mean they won't so give it a go, mess and all. Not forgetting seasoning. We definitely omit salt from our diet so I'm certainly not giving it to my cherubs but black pepper is a delight for them and can give that bland food the little extra it needs; the same is true of ginger, garlic and lemongrass. Try them as a soup base or within your chicken stock.

The world of weaning equipment seems to be designed to fill your kitchen from floor to ceiling in my opinion; weaning spoons for example are fabulous but what's wrong with a teaspoon or a cereal bowl rather than the fancy coloured baby weaning bowl? Invest heavily on what you'll use long term but mainly use what you already have. Does baby really know the difference between a pretty weaning bowl and a ramekin, and if they did, do they actually care? Bibs are a must and disposable ones too if you can get them. Always keep at least one in the car with a ready pouch of organic food for that odd emergency that does happen, such as the car breaking down or the three hour unexpected traffic jam. This way at least you can stop and feed baby and pop in to see friends unplanned, as you always used to as you've got everything with you. Keep the same in the change bag too as the one day you don't take it that's when the car really will break down.

The other really useful item I find is flannels at feeding time. I mean the ten for £1 ones. Have a huge box of the cheapy ones you can get from any store and dampen one when you make baby's food, then you can clean their face up with it afterwards then the highchair before sterilising so the worst of the mess is gone and it's softer than a baby wipe and quicker. Then just bung the flannels in the wash with the bedding when done.

Highchairs are easy though, when baby's got their food everywhere, all over them, the straps, the sides, the cover, the tray and places you never knew were there; how easy is it to clean and keep clean? Again why buy this when baby's three months? Why not, when baby arrives and if suitable from birth pop baby in to watch you from the very start when you cook. Baby will feel part of the family at meal times with a couple of little toys to play with or look at, they'll be happier and you can eat in peace. It's a false economy waiting, as is true of the travel cot as you can get so much use out of them from when baby is tiny not just when the manufacturer says so.

The highchair will need a tray that can go in the dishwasher, a tray you can adjust and remove one handed and one that fits in your space. Watch this as in the shop they really are deceptive and don't look as big as they really are so get the tape measure out. We've got quite a large highchair and mostly it stays in the kitchen so Sophia can bang spoons and watch me whilst I cook; also after feeding the kitchen floor is far easier to clean than the cream carpet. As well as this highchair, we also have a plastic one that pops on any chair, so Sophia can come into any room with me now and if I have a late bath after taking the dog for a walk then this chair will come into the bathroom too, sort of like the swing did. It just keeps her in view and out of the little mischief she seems to find. A few crackers keep her happy for ages now she's a little older. An adjustable back rest is also very important, so it can be adjusted depending on the child's strength and age but don't be conned with the marketing of it turning into a toddler chair as by this time they should be no doubt sitting on a normal chair at the table with you, not being treated like a baby still.

Gosh I did have more to say on this than I first thought, but a handful of vegetables out of the Sunday roast and a good highchair and you're set. Weaning sorted.

PART FIVE
The Essentials…no frills

Equipment

The change bag is one of the most important items of baby equipment for a woman you'll ever buy. You'll use it every day and it needs to be multi-functional too as its now your handbag, but you don't want to emasculate your partner when they're out on their own either. Technically there's a wide choice and with our first and second girls, I did have fancy change bags but this time I knew exactly what I required.

I don't warm baby milk, so I didn't need the expensive thermal pockets or coin holder. I needed a bag with minimum two external pockets, one for a bottle of milk and one for my keys, phone and purse. Inside though, I just needed something almost like a sack, as my baby wipes had their own container and I used a plastic zip sandwich bag for the change mat, nappy sacks and nappies; as this way there's no washing involved and once a week I just chuck out the plastic bags and replace with a clean one. I also have a plastic bag with that essential change of clothes and blanket, as that can keep the girls warm or double up as a play mat and then another bag of food, bib, a milk portioner, and spoon. There are lots of plastic bags, but it keeps everything clean and dry and easy to reach and you can identify the essentials immediately.

I also needed to make sure the change bag could fit by the girl's feet in the car and that the handle was suitable to go over the pushchair handle and be adjustable, so both myself and my partner could carry it comfortably. So a fancy £200 bag wasn't for me this time, just a cute and practical everyday bag works for us! Stop and think a moment; what am I actually getting for my money? What's making it different from a normal everyday large bag? Apart from the price is there a real difference?

As I've previously said, this manual isn't all about the equipment, but it wouldn't be complete without my list of baby must haves for our family. These are the essentials we needed, however do note how long baby actually uses them for and put your funds into the area you feel requires the investment as not all of us can afford everything we want for baby. This is what we really needed before the girls arrived and nothing more. Everything else we worked out after to stop us wasting money unnecessarily on clothes and swanky gadgets.

The List

Crib (not swinging or gliding)

Crib sheets – 2 x flat 2 x fitted

Swaddling x 2

Sleeping bag (from about three months)

Baby bath towel hooded x 2

Muslin cloths x12

Disposable change mats

Disposable bibs

Feeding flannels x 6

Baby bath

Foam bath support

Bath thermometer

Bibs x 6

Calpol

Ashton & Parsons – powder for teething

Organic baby wash

Hand held blender

Ice cube tray

Wardrobe

Chest of drawers

Travel cot plus 2 fitted sheets

Mattress protector for cot

Baskets for bootees, hats, socks

Cot

Cot sheets - 2 x fitted sheets

Weaning spoons

Sandwich bags for food cubes

Steriliser

Bottles

Baby milk

Milk portioner

Change bag
Change mat – disposable and cot top
Baby monitor
Baby car seat
Highchair
Baby swing
Play blanket
Play Arch – ensure sturdy and can add or detach toys
Car sun blinds
Pushchair
Zip up plastic bags for in change bag
Nappies
Nappy sacks
Wipes
Shawl for bringing baby home
Blankets x 3

The clothing must haves…

Newborn size…
2 x vests
2 x cardigans
4 x baby grows
1 small hat
2 pairs socks
2 pairs mittens
1x premature size baby grow and 1x 0-3 months

You'll never know until baby arrives the size of clothes you really need and don't remove the labels. We had loads in the wrong size that needed to go back to the shops. What are useful, I've found, are the starter sets consisting of hat, bib, light jacket, vest and baby grow. It all comes as a bundle and it all matches. It's hard not to buy all those cute clothes and I haven't managed to completely stop myself, but we had to return so so much again and do you keep all your receipts? Treat yourself to those little baby indulgences by all means, but not every time you leave the house. Can you really afford for baby to never, and I mean never wear the items? It's strange how baby changes you and you become all gooey over anything tiny but hold back!!

Honestly this is all you need to start, but be prepared to go shopping quite soon after baby arrives, but at least you'll be buying the right size now not guessing and they will all be completely justified purchases, as you will know if baby needs more cardigans because it's a little chilly out or if hats really aren't needed because it's so warm. The wait will be worth it.

The way it is, our way

I've only touched upon some of the areas that new parents face. It's crazy to think how one little person changes your world entirely and how they can make you feel totally inadequate whilst doing the most important job there is, but every smile makes us remember why we do it and why we want to do it.

The truth of the matter is we all muddle through and eventually find our own way. Not because we know what we're doing, but because we have to. No-one else is going to choose the pushchair for us or put baby to bed or change the sticky green gloopy pooey nappy. We have to do it on our own and at best, as part of a family. I just want to put it out there…why don't we all start being honest with each other and start sharing how bringing up baby really is? Not the theory or the role model way, but the reality of day to day me and baby.

I admit there are two books I couldn't live without which are 'What to expect when you're expecting' by Arlene Eisenberg any edition and the 'Yummy mummy and me cookbook' by Hope Ricciotti. The first made me think about what's actually happening, how and why and answered all my pre-natal questions no matter how stupid they really were and the latter made me look at eating in a whole new capacity and gave our family some new recipe ideas which made a difference to our family meal times. When I felt like everyone was telling me I could hardly eat a thing because it was bad for baby, I had the facts thanks to this book. Don't go overboard with food and go health mad when pregnant, just be sensible and having everything in moderation kind of sums it up. I haven't mentioned these books elsewhere in this manual because I didn't want to repeat their content, as they cover the pre-natal and pregnancy eating so thoroughly and detail all prior to baby's arrival in a way far better than I could ever hope to. The secrets to once baby's in your arms are found in this manual, well I hope they can be found here anyway.

I do hope you enjoyed your coffee and have taken a moment to revive and get some peace. Mostly though, I hope you feel comforted that you're not the only one making it all up as you go along and that we all have those tear your hair out moments, but they are more than outweighed by those beautiful smiles and giggles back. Children turn our worlds upside down and change our lives in ways unimaginable to a non-parent. What we don't realise is, that it's these changes which make our lives richer. I couldn't and wouldn't be without our angels (or terrors depending on the day of the week you ask me).

Note to parents

It definitely is hard being a parent without doubt, but as soon as you've mastered them being a baby and you've bumbled through and found a daily routine that works, it all changes. It doesn't change a little bit, but massively. Your little treasure starts to walk opening a world or terror for all parents no matter how experienced. You can no longer put them on the floor to play without having eyes in the back of your head. To make things even more challenging they learn to talk and then you have to work out potty training.

The hardest bit of all though, arrives when they're around 3 years old. Do you put them in a nursery environment or pre-school? Does the ratio of boys to girls matter to you? What do you do if you don't gel with the teacher but your child does? How involved do you want to be with your child's school? If you go back to work, can you still make the moments of singing on stage, sports day and scariest of all parents evening?

Just as you feel comfortable, your world will be tossed up in the air and re-jigged from top to bottom when you have children. It's always hard, it never gets easier, and you just find a way to muddle through. You will find a way to answer those all important questions at every stage of your child's life; it just takes time and a little confidence. Confidence to know that the decisions you make are the right ones for your family.

Your family is the most important thing in your world and if like me, as soon as you think you have it figured out you'll have another little addition to the family. Then it all starts again…how are we going to manage? Where are they going to sleep? Can we really still do this? Are we strong enough as a family? Where do you find the ability to love another like your first? And you will manage, you do have boundless stores of love that keep giving and you will find the perfect way to become a family all over again.

To be good parents you just require a strong ability to cope with change and you need to be prepared for the uncertain. There are so many surprises along the journey of parenthood and I've found that mostly the surprises make me smile. It's the surprise of their first word or first drawing home from school. Every hug from our girls reminds me, they remind me we are doing an okay job; even if I'm not Superwoman and we are making it all up as we go along day by day.

Disclaimer

This manual is the sole opinion of the author. The information within this manual is not meant to be used and should not be used to diagnose or treat any medical or psychological conditions. For a medical diagnosis, you should consult with your physician.

The author and publisher are in no way liable for damages caused or allegedly caused either directly or indirectly by the information contained within this manual. Any treatment, action or application to any person reading the information herein is not at the liability of the author or publisher, but the individual.

All information, references to products and books do not in any way, in part or in full constitute endorsement.

The author is not a health professional or feeding expert and professional advice should always be sought for all health and feeding concerns. You are solely responsible for your own choices, your own actions and the results as a consequence.

About the author

Katy Handley graduated from Leeds Metropolitan University with BA (Hons) Economics for Business and from Bournemouth University with MSc Finance and Law. She is a progressive hands-on mother, inspired to write for those facing parenthood in the modern world.

Representing a new wave of thinking surrounding motherhood, Katy makes it known that you don't need to be Superwoman and that parents are normal everyday people that do not necessarily have all the answers.

Katy's career path has taken a diversion from the managerial role she played within retail finance and demonstrates how a practical, logical approach to being a homemaker can be just as demanding and rewarding as a business role. She lives a life buzzing with energy and activity together with her partner, three children and her dog in Hampshire.

Katy's other works include

SIMPLE ELEGANCE
The Big Little Homemade Gift Bible

For all your family, friend, teacher, children and pet
gifts made from the heart. It's a perfect solution for all
occasions; filled with a beautiful collection of gifts that
you really can make yourself.

Available online 2011